DISCLAIMER

THIS BOOK IS NOT DESIGNED TO, AND DOES NOT, PROVIDE MEDICAL ADVICE. ALL CONTENT ("CONTENT"), INCLUDING TEXT, GRAPHICS, IMAGES AND INFORMATION AVAILABLE IN OR THROUGH THIS BOOK ARE FOR GENERAL INFORMATIONAL PURPOSES ONLY.

THE CONTENT IS NOT INTENDED TO BE A SUBSTITUTE FOR PROFESSIONAL MEDICAL ADVICE, DIAGNOSIS OR TREATMENT. NEVER DISREGARD PROFESSIONAL MEDICAL ADVICE, OR DELAY IN SEEKING IT, BECAUSE OF SOMETHING YOU HAVE READ ON THIS BOOK. NEVER RELY ON INFORMATION ON THIS BOOK IN PLACE OF SEEKING PROFESSIONAL MEDICAL ADVICE.

THE AUTHOR, PUBLISHER AND ALL AFFILIATED PARTIES ARE NOT RESPONSIBLE OR LIABLE FOR ANY ADVICE, COURSE OF TREATMENT, DIAGNOSIS OR ANY OTHER INFORMATION, SERVICES OR PRODUCTS THAT YOU OBTAIN THROUGH THIS SITE. YOU ARE ENCOURAGED TO CONFER WITH YOUR DOCTOR WITH REGARD TO INFORMATION CONTAINED IN OR THROUGH THIS BOOK. AFTER READING THIS BOOK, YOU ARE ENCOURAGED TO REVIEW THE INFORMATION CAREFULLY WITH YOUR PROFESSIONAL HEALTHCARE PROVIDER.

LIMITATION OF LIABILITY

Table of Contents

And It Starts...

"But mommy, I don't want to go to daycare! I want to stay with you!"

Words so familiar, they're practically an anthem for a generation of dual income households, as is the inevitable next line (sing it with me, if you know the lyrics):

"I'd like that, too, sweetie, but it just isn't an option right now. We can't afford to do that."

Heartbreaking words that remind us that the good old days really are over, and that we can't raise our next generation with the same attention to values and family interconnectedness that our parents and grandparents raised our parents and us on...

......or can we?

Today's modern world offers a variety of daycare options for young children and their families, and you might be surprised at what some of those options are.

As a parent, what are some of my options? How can I be sure that I'm leaving my child in the best hands possible? After all, the whole reason that I need some sort of childcare service is that I'm going to be at work all day, and the reason that I'm going to be at work all day is so that I can pay the rent and buy food for my family.

If I'm going to work this hard providing the good things in life for my children, I really need to start by figuring out what the best fit is for my own personal childcare needs. Will Heather be safe if I bring her to a drop in center, or would a pre-school be better equipped to handle her potentially fatal peanut allergies? Will Nick learn the social skills he will need to know later in life if I hire an au pair? Will Lisa be bullied by the other kids if I send her to an in home childcare center? Is William old enough for a daycare?

I also need to watch out for any red flags that may pop up while I'm looking for childcare services in different forms. For example, in the scenario above where we are worried about little Lisa being bullied, finding out if an in home childcare center is licensed will go a long way towards solving that riddle. Licensed in home childcare centers have to meet with strict government regulations, and comply with mandatory public education policies such as anti-bullying laws. The same rigidity of standards is not necessarily present in an unlicensed in home childcare facility.

The list of the most popular options, in the order that they will be discussed in, is as follows:

1) Corporate childcare provided by a place of work. (if available),
2) Family members helping out (if available).
3) In- home childcare (licensed or unlicensed).
4) Preschool (Head Start programs, limited vouchers for public, fees for private).
5) Daycare (The traditional choice for dual income families).
6) Au pair/ nanny (Live in or not, pricing break for room-and-board makes affordable)
7) Stay at home (w/ mommy's helper) (loss of income, best emotional choice for kid?)
8) Drop in centers (Flexible but less personal, kids vary over time, policies).

9) Childcare Co-ops (collection of childcare resources)
10) Cyber-nanny (a bad idea, brought to you by the tech generation).

Now that we have our list composed, let's take some time to go through what each of the options are, and some of the benefits and concessions that are necessary for each one.

Remember, childcare is about the child, and, like snowflakes, no two kids are exactly alike. Finding the right fit for you child is far more important than taking the advice of those who seek to tell you which method is "better" than the others. After all, it's better to clear away snow with a snow plow, isn't it? Not if the snow melts. Being young and new to this world, children take their behavioral cues from the people around them, so it's often hard to tell how much is the child's original thought, and what is simply parroting. This inadvertent deception often makes water look like snow, and can have disastrous consequences - just look at the reasons that the anti-bullying laws became necessary to implement in the first place!

For example, a child with a high IQ and who shows some early signs of being socially charismatic might thrive in preschool, but that same child may well feel limited if left at home with an au pair. A different child, for the sake of example we'll say she's just as intelligent but needs to work on her social skills, might prefer going to museums and learning from an au pair, who can, one on one, slowly indoctrinate the child into the world of social interaction. The key is to find out what your child needs, and then to shape your childcare choices around those needs.

Corporate Child Care Provided By a Place of Work

It used to be common practice for multiple generations of people to live in the same house, and to set up neighborhoods according to ethnic similarity, giving the neighbors a sense of interconnectedness because they shared similar cultural values. There are some places where this is still the common practice: for example, the Portuguese population near Cape Cod is very interconnected, and values are shared and enforced by everyone in the Portuguese community in New Bedford.

I recently had an experience in New Bedford that illustrated this phenomena. I was at a garage getting a tune up and an oil change, and the mechanic said "usually the man pays for the car" when my boyfriend and I squabbled in a friendly way over the bill. This mechanic, who happened to be male himself, said this while making eye contact with me, and the look on his face said "woman, know your place."

Not being part of the native Portuguese population in New Bedford, Mass, I got offended. I kept right on feeling offended by this incident, and relating it in story to other friends of mine, until it was explained to me by one of these friends that in the Portuguese sub culture in New Bedford, women are expected to live in their father's homes until they get married, at which point they are then considered to be living in their husbands' homes. There is no point where a woman owns property, so it makes no sense for her to pay for something, since she'd be using her father's or husband's money anyway. This doesn't mean that women in the Portuguese sub culture of New Bedford don't work, but it does mean that they turn over thier paychecks to husbands and fathers, who use them for family bills etc. Home cleaning allowances and personal allowances are commonplace for women, and a woman's personal allowance isn't expected to stretch into paying for things like auto repair or the electric bill.

So, as difficult as if was for me to understand at the time, the mechanic who corrected my socially maladaptive behavior (socially maladaptive in the specific Portuguese community in New Bedford where my car was being worked on) wasn't trying to be rude, he was trying to give me what he saw as a very important social cue that I was committing a faux pas, and he was trying to bring me back to my senses by butting into the seeming argument with my male counterpart, who for all he knew might very well be my husband.

This is the type of thing they mean when they say "it takes a village to raise a child." Reading this example is bound to have some parents nodding along in understanding at the traditional tone of the values, while other readers of this booklet are getting red-faced in angry disgust at the sexism inherent in my example. This very difference of response illustrates the point that I am trying to make. Whatever your values are, instill them in your child in a conscious way, or the values of the immediate culture that they live in will be instilled in thier place. For many people, thier values reflect family values that were instilled in them as children, and, if this is the care, grand parents and other blood relations might be the best answer to the question of childcare services during the parents' work day.

Again, it used to be the norm to house multiple generations of a family in the same house, with the older generation dying off so that the younger could take up ownership of the property at that time. While it is a less prevalent practice today, this traditional home composition does still exist in some ethnic sub cultures.

Often, since they're living under the same roof, grandmothers will take care of little ones while their moms go off to work, and no one thinks anything of it, it's just the natural, normal way of things. If you're fortunate enough to be living in a situation where your family is babysitting for free "because you're family [and so is the child]" take some advice and don't look a gift horse in the mouth. Not only will the child be protected and cared for by individuals who love him or her and care very much about his or her best interests, but he or she will be getting behavioral cues from the culture that he or she is going to grow up in, and that ability to communicate clearly and be understood by those closest to you is valuable on its own.

As said before, different children thrive and wilt in different situations, and so if you feel very strongly that your child should, say, go to preschool, where there will be more varied social interaction with peers from his or her own age group, then yes, go with your gut; you're the parent and it's your call to make. All I'm trying to say is don't overlook the obvious benefits before rejecting any childcare option.

Family Members Helping Out

In home childcare comes in both licensed and unlicensed forms, and the difference between the two can be large. In the next section of this booklet, we will explore some of the advantages and disadvantages of each of the two options, and learn how to spot red flags in an in home childcare environment.

In home childcare is an arrangement for services between a parent or parents and a childcare worker who has set up his or her home to be child-safe and child-friendly, because it will contain a given group of children congregating there on a daily basis.

Unlike a childcare drop in center, most in home childcare involves the same children coming back day after day, so that friendships and other social bonds can be forged, and an expected daily routine can form. The literature shows that routine is a soothing agent for many children, as the security and predictability can have a calming effect on children who are otherwise prone to temper tantrums and erratic behavior, because the chaos that leads to a chaotic reaction is replaced by stability in the child's environment.

Many in home childcare centers are created by people who themselves have children, and who decided to earn some money, instead of spending it, spending time with their child or children during the work day. In some cases, the income is extra money, and in some cases, the income accrued is rent money. Whether the childcare worker is volunteering his or her own personal space for childcare services for financial or strictly emotional reasons will have a direct bearing on the price of childcare. Additionally, licensed centers usually, but not always, charge a little bit more for services, and homes with toy, play scapes, story corners, etc plainly visible -aka, home that are clearly set up for the business of in home childcare- will also charge slightly higher rates.

All in home childcare centers are not created equal, and one very prominent sign of quality is whether the particular home care venue is licensed or not. As mentioned, this will be discussed in it's own section, in part two of this booklet. Until then, think about what licensure is: a government's thumb's up to a particular person or venue for a particular service or product. What might be a benefit of government oversight in a childcare situation? What kinds of standards would it be reasonable to expect from an in home childcare environment? What might earn a frown, or a thumbs down reaction, and would you be willing to potentially expose your child to those situations?

In-home Child Care

In home child care comes in both licensed and unlicensed forms, and the difference between the two can be large. In the next section of this booklet, we will explore some of the advantages and disadvantages of each of the two options, and learn how to spot red flags in an in home child care environment.

In home child care is an arrangement for services between a parent or parents and a child care worker who has set up his or her home to be child-safe and child-friendly, because it will contain a given group of children congregating there on a daily basis.

Unlike a child care drop in center, most in home child care involves the same children coming back day after day, so that friendships and other social bonds can be forged, and an expected daily routine can form. The literature shows that routine is a soothing agent for many children, as the security and predictability can have a calming effect on children who are otherwise prone to temper tantrums and erratic behavior, because the chaos that leads to a chaotic reaction is replaced by stability in the child's environment.

Many in home child care centers are created by people who themselves have children, and who decided to earn some money, instead of spending it, spending time with their child or children during the work day. In some cases, the income is extra money, and in some cases, the income accrued is rent money. Whether the child care worker is volunteering his or her own personal space for child care services for financial or strictly emotional reasons will have a direct bearing on the price of child care. Additionally, licensed centers usually, but not always, charge a little bit more for services, and homes with toy, play scapes, story corners, etc plainly visible -aka, home that are clearly set up for the business of in home child care- will also charge slightly higher rates.

All in home child care centers are not created equal, and one very prominent sign of quality is whether the particular home care venue is licensed or not. As mentioned, this will be discussed in it's own section, in part two of this booklet. Until then, think about what licensure is: a government's thumb's up to a particular person or venue for a particular service or product. What might be a benefit of government oversight in a child care situation? What kinds of standards would it be reasonable to expect from an in home child care environment? What might earn a frown, or a thumbs down reaction, and would you be willing to potentially expose your child to those situations?

Preschool

Preschool becomes an option when your child turns 3 or 4, and there are many factors that go in to selecting a preschool environment, or even when deciding whether or not to send your child to preschool at all, or to wait until kindergarten, when school becomes mandatory.

In the interest of helping children in urban areas where the socio-economic climate is lower income than suburban areas tend to be, the government has instituted programs such as Head Start, limited vouchers for public preschools that fall into the top tiers when the schools are rated, and, in rare cases, the waiving of fees for private preschools.

The Department of Children and Families, the same people who are in charge of Women, Infants, and Children (WIC) food programs, are available to answer questions and provide information on these programs, as well as get your child's name onto a waiting list if applicable. It is a good idea to put your child's name on a waiting list, even if you haven't made a final decision yet, if you are leaning towards preschool for your child, since you can always waive your right to use a voucher if you've decided against it, but it is very hard to get a voucher at the last minute.

If you are not in a lower socio economic strata, the financial cost of private preschools should be measured against the services that the individual private preschool offers. What kind of preparation for elementary school do they supply? The best answer to this question is that they teach kids the basics that they will need to know in order to keep up with the rest of the class, both academically and socially, when they get to kindergarten What elementary school a parent is planning on sending their child to, should have a direct impact on which preschool is chosen as preparation. What kinds of schools do graduates of this private preschool go on to, and do they bloom or fade in that elementary environment?

For example, say you want to send your child to Bates Preschool, a place that assumes that their children will continue on with kindergarten at Bates Elementary School, and further education will stay privatized all the way through Bates High School, which is a privately-funded boarding school completely outside of the public sector. If a child does go through the entire Bates education, the cost of all those years of private education might well rival the cost of sending your 18 year old to a four year college, so budget has to be considered.

Many parents fall into the trap of thinking that private schooling is always the better choice, even if it has to be interrupted due to financial restraints. "We'll send Amy to Bates through 5th grade," a parent might say, "after that, she'll just have to learn how to keep doing well in a public school." Because of this misapplication of logic, Amy's parents are willing to shell out the big bucks for private preschool, only to have Amy experience a culture shock when she enters the local public Jr High School, which will likely have many more students, less one on one teacher-student interaction, and a completely different set of social values from her new peers than the ones she had become used to at Bates. This type of change to a new school environment can be daunting to try to navigate, even if Amy is fully prepared for the change.

In cases such as Amy's, a better choice might be to save the money that would have been spent on Bates through the elementary years in a college account, and look into the local public and lower priced private elementary schools that are available to Amy.

Many times, Catholic schools offer privatized education at a fraction of the cost of non-religious private schools, and many other religions are beginning to develop educational plans that involve religious schooling. Additionally, many school zones offer a choice of public schools, depending on which ones a child lives near, with a voucher program for children who live far away from some of the top rated ones, but still want to get that level of education. Magnet schools offer half-day specialized schooling for the child who qualifies in writing, theater, dance, science, mathematics, and so on. Finally, Montessori and learner-centered schools offer children completely alternative education that has been shown to increase creativity and show comparable SAT scores when the primary education is completed, and college looms on the horizon.

This whole process begins with preschool, or childcare in lieu of preschool. The most important thing to take into account when choosing what to do is to assess what your child will need to know (social skills from interaction with peers is a huge learning need for this age group) to progress to the next level of education, as each level of education is completed.

Daycare

Daycare is the traditional childcare choice for dual income families. Several different types of daycare exist, but the fundamental difference between daycare and other options (such as mother's helpers and baby sitters) is that daycare is a steady, reliable option for childcare that opens the children involved to learning social cues and age appropriate social behavior, since it takes place by putting several kids into one room and keeping them there.

Most daycares have a learning element, although this element might not be as prominent as it is in a preschool environment. For example, there might be building blocks and story time, but no pre-k curriculum set out specifically for the kids to follow.

There are several types of childcare available today, such as drop off centers, in home care (which is becoming increasingly popular, and which is discussed in detail later in this booklet), preschool, and so on. There are several questions parents should ask before leaving their child in any childcare environment, but these questions are especially relevant to a daycare environment, where the structure is usually much more fixed, or set in stone, than it might be in other childcare environments.

Question #1: What are the hours of operation?

Daycare centers usually have specific hours of operation that are intended to give parents with "normal" 9:00 am to 5:00 pm jobs enough time to drop their kids off, get to work, work, drive to daycare from work, and pick their kids up. Some daycares are open until 7:00 pm or later, due to travel times involved in the parents' process, but some close at 5:30 pm or 6:00 pm, so be sure to inquire about closing times and plan your route from work accordingly. Most daycares open between 7:00 am and 8:00 am, with a rare few opening as early as 6:00 am or 6:30 am.

It is important to choose a daycare center whose hours correspond with your pick up and drop off availability, otherwise you might be left without childcare because of being "late" for pickup too many times.

Question #2: Where is the daycare center located?

In addition to factoring in time to commute from home to daycare to work and back again, it is a good idea to get a feel for where a daycare center is relative to your home. Does little Suzie have to spend more time in the car, which makes her car sick, than is absolutely necessary, in order to get to daycare? Is the daycare center local to your home neighborhood, which is a social advantage when it comes to setting up play dates among the children? Neighborhood local daycare is also a community wide social advantage in terms of being likely to have the types of values you would prefer be instilled in your child, considering the fact that you chose, as an adult to live in your neighborhood and to some degree support local values.

An additional advantage of daycare centers is that some are corporate conglomerates, which is an advantage because it becomes a seamless process to move your child from one of their centers to another one in the same corporate family, with all your child's allergy information, medical needs, potty routines, etc traveling with him or her, in the event of a family move. There are no guarantees that there will be another daycare center in the area you are moving to, of course, but finding out about satellite centers when enrolling your child in daycare is a smart way to stay on top of the potential transitions as much as possible.

Question #3: Is it licensed?

We go into a lot of detail in this booklet about why in home care centers should be licensed, and the point is doubled for a corporate daycare center. Usually, daycare centers are licensed institutions, and a rule of thumb is that if a daycare center is unlicensed, it is an unsafe environment for your child to be in. This is because of professional expectations for daycare centers specifically, whereas in an in home center an unlicensed situation may be acceptable, if not optimal, so long as the right questions are asked and answered to your satisfaction. It's very hard for a daycare center to defend or explain away not having a license, however, and if one makes a good show of it, chances are it's still not a good idea to leave your child at an unlicensed daycare center.

Question #4: What are the workers like?

Simply, is your child in an environment where the workers who interact with him or her over the course of the day are qualified and behaviorally appropriate for the environment? We all know the obvious things, such as swearing childcare worker who haven't bathed or shaved in a week are a big bad red flag, and this question is addressing that which we already know.

If your gut tells you that a particular person shouldn't be anywhere near your child, then your child shouldn't be anywhere near that person. Conversely, if your gut tells you that a particular worker is a nurturing, positive influence on your child, green light the daycare and find out what that worker's shifts tend to be.

Parents have natural instincts about people and environments that interact with their offspring, even if they can't place a finger on a description, or give words to the warnings. If your gut tells you something about your childcare environment or worker, listen to it.

Question #5: What is the parental visit policy?

Much like in the corporate childcare and in home childcare environments, the policy at a daycare should be open arms when a parent chooses to visit his or her child during the day. If there is a delay in opening the door, or if the center is less than accommodating when you'd like to see your child, this is a major red flag.

However, if the daycare center does welcome you in, some things to check for during your visit are how your child is interacting with the other children (non-interaction with his or her peers might be a signal that bullying or social ostracism of your child is occurring, which is a situation that must be nipped in the bud as soon as it is found out); how comfortable your child is telling the worker that he or she needs to go potty, or proudly showing off a finger painting, or asking for a snack (children thrive in healthy environments, so a comfortable child to worker interaction is a good sign that the workers are doing their jobs properly); and how comfortable your child is overall in the environment of the daycare center (while it is normal to be a little intimidated at first, your child should soon ease into a routine at daycare that puts him or her at ease, and allows the natural joy and curiosity that is found in the pre-k stage of childhood to bloom).

In addition to watching for your child's specific reactions and interactions at the daycare, you should also keep an eye out for confirmation that the workers that you spoke to pre enrollment were being honest about the facilities you chose to go with. Is the finger paint station neat and clean, with the small paint jars lidded and closed up tightly? Is there a finger painting station at all, if one was promised? What about the potato stamps; are any of them rotting or growing green shoots? Are there any unwashed sponges growing mold cultures without the aid of petri dishes? Is there a stack of dirty diapers overflowing the trash can, spilling out onto the floor? While these examples may seem absurd and extreme, the point stands that the daycare center should actively and obviously live up to the promises that it made when you were looking at childcare options.

Au Pair or Nanny

An au pair is a person who lives in your home and takes over some domestic duties, including childcare, in exchange for room-and-board, a small stipend, and help learning the native language of the land the au pair is living and working in. Many families come to see their au pair as a member of the family, and the benefits of having your childcare worker living in the same house as you and your kids are immeasurable when it comes to consistency of care and availability of childcare services.

An additional benefit to having your childcare worker live in your house is found during the morning routine. The hardest time of day for small children is often the time when their parents must part from them, dropping them off at daycare or preschool. With an au pair, there is no traumatic (in the child's mind) parting; instead, the au pair, which the children eventually view as a member of the family, much like a favorite aunt or uncle, simply picks up where the parents leave off when it's time for them to go to work.

Usually, an au pair's job includes helping out with cooking and cleaning, and other domestic chores, kind of like a "mommy's helper" but without the supervision element. Ensuring that the children do their homework and finish their own chores is part of these domestic responsibilities, as is teaching them how to get and keep their own rooms clean and tidy.

While the au pair's responsibilities are numerous, they are not limitless. Discussing what boundaries there are between the family and the au pair, such as family members not being allowed past the closed door of the au pair's room; negotiating a weekly day off, or weekly time off if a whole day is impossible; and working with an au pair who is taking classes part time while she or he is in the country, are all part of the overall experience of both the family and the au pair during their time together.

While the au pair is living in the house, there is a cultural learning and educational enrichment opportunity for your children through interaction with this person from a foreign country. There is also an opportunity for the adults in the household to learn about another culture and broaden their knowledge base about social customs and common practices in places outside of their own country. This opportunity for all members of the family is returned to the au pair, who is able to experience American culture firsthand by working as an au pair.

The difference between a nanny and an au pair is that a nanny may or may not live in the house with the children, and a traditional nanny isn't a student from another land looking for a cultural enrichment experience, but rather a normal American looking for a childcare job. There will be no language barrier with a traditional nanny, who may well have lived his or her entire life down the street from the house he or she's been hired at. Nannies are also typically more expensive than au pairs, and have been typecast as a care giving alternative for people in higher socioeconomic strata who can afford their services.

Much like an au pair, a nanny will care for children in the childrens' own home, overseeing the child's emotional, social, and physical development. Because a nanny is working only with the child or children of one household, she or he will become well versed in things like food or bee allergies, parent-approved snacks and entertainment, and so on.

A nanny is also in a one on one relationship with the child or children in his or her care, and this relationship usually puts the child or children at ease when it is time to talk to the adult in charge about personal issues. As with an au pair, nannies are usually expected to take on a few domestic responsibilities during their time at work, such as light house cleaning and preparing meals for the children.

If you get a nanny from an agency, which is the recommended way to hire a nanny, she or he will be background checked and drug screened, to ensure that she or he has no criminal background or history of substance abuse. Generally, potential au pairs are checked out the same way, when they join up with the over seas program that they sign their contract with.

One final advantage of going with a nanny or an au pair is the flexibility that comes with making your own schedule. At a daycare facility, for example, the children might not nap for as long as you would like, or your child might not fall asleep until the end of nap time. At home, the nanny or au pair directly oversees napping habits and institutes the times and durations for naps. This is one example of tailor made scheduling; others might include other events in the day to day routine, which, when overseen by one person who isn't flooded with children to oversee, can become a very specific and personal series of events, which turn into a tailor made routine.

Stay At Home (With Mommy's Helper)

Even for mothers and fathers who are fully employed, there are corporate options, such as maternal and paternal leave, that can help out by freeing up time when the child is first born. This is the time to discuss options and preferences. If you and your partner have discussed your roles as parents and breadwinners, and have decided that the family can make do with just one income, then the option of being a stay at home mom or a stay at home dad opens up, depending on who is keeping their job.

The first thing we need to look at when we make the decision to have one parent -either the mom or the dad- stay at home, in a dual income household, is what kind of impact that loss of a second income will have upon the family. In many cases, it's simply not a real option, and here we have the realm of the work-at-home mom or dad and the "mother's helper" assistant, which can ease the burden by allowing the parent who stays at home to still earn money for the household, albeit in a different way than before.

It has been recommended to do things such as select an unused room and turn it into a work-at-home office, get a second phone line and a private answering machine that is separate from the family line, and install wireless internet, either has high speed DSL or Broadband, in order to help the home environment transform into a work environment as well. These are all good suggestions, provided the overhead for getting them in the first place is there. If not, many people make do with a cell phone devoted to the business that is always on, and a web page. Depending on what type of at-home business you'll be running, you may need different things to get started and to keep it up.

One such thing that may be of use is a "mother's helper" intern.

What a "mother's helper" is, is a college student in the childcare field, performing an internship with your family in order to complete needed practicum credits. Often the services of the intern are free, since this is a learning experience for him or her, and having a helper can be a great advantage when trying to juggle laundry, house cleaning, cooking dinner, playing with the kids, getting those forms filled out, setting up the internet account for the at-home office, and buying a toy moose that's suitable for ages 3 and under, because it was recommended now that the baby is teething, before getting dinner ready for the whole family by 6:00 pm.

The "mother's helper's" unpaid job is exactly what it sounds like: of the above list, the mother (or father) who lives and works at home, will choose what tasks he or she really needs to do personally. The other tasks, if they are doable in a single day, will be the day's quota for the helper. Unlike baby sitters, helpers are directly supervised by the parent who is working from home, which creates a different dynamic in the relationship.

Since the whole point of staying at home is to be able to raise your child yourself, and, since caring for a living, breathing child is such a fluctuating activity, with things rarely going according to plan (boo-boos and oopses happen), it is important for both the parent and the helper to be flexible in their expectations for the day. While the parent is (of course) the one in charge, open dialogue and communication between parent and helper will make for a more successful relationship. This success will enrich the helper's experience during his or her internship, and it will make day to day life much easier for both helper and parent during that internship.

Some mother's helpers don't go to school, they are simply people who are paid a salary to come in to work each day, or who live with the family and take room, board, and a stipend instead of higher education credits as their payment for being mother's helpers. This way of choosing to use people who are mother's helpers as a career path, instead of interns who are helping for the experience while moving forward in the field of childcare, can be less cost-effective than utilizing interns, but may lead to longer term employment, in which the mother's helper begins to resemble an au pair, in that they are seen as a member of the family.

When nursing, they say "breast is best" when comparing the nutritional value of breast milk and formulas. Does the same principle hold true when it comes to care giving? Is it truly the best option to raise a child alone, at home, instead of in a social environment with other children?

Social skills learned by preschool aged children carry over into the rest of their lives. So, if you do choose to raise a child at home, be sure to include an agenda with opportunities for social interaction, such as swimming lessons (when your child is old enough) or other similar activities for kids in the same age group as your child.

Another alternative, which will be gone into in greater detail in other sections of this book, is choosing to stay at home and raise you child, while working as an in-home care provider. This might be a fantastic option, as it allows your child the daily social interaction that is recommended for preschool aged children, and it also allows you to bond with your child on a daily basis, while still earning money to keep the household afloat.

Drop in centers

Even though they are emergency childcare services for last-minute childcare needs, drop in centers often require pre-registration paperwork be filled out before a child is dropped off, and it is a good idea to register your child early, so that you can use the service as it was intended when the time comes. Some drop-in centers are exclusively drop-in in nature, while others are regular daycare centers with drop in options.

Always expect extra fees when utilizing emergency childcare, and please note that many drop-in centers charge registration fees up front, in addition to other charges. Additional fees above and beyond the initial emergency childcare fees could include an extra charge for children who are still present (and therefore must be cared for) after a drop-in center closes for the day, an extra charge for holiday childcare and weekend childcare, and extra item charges such as diapers and snacks.

Very often, a drop-in daycare center will have a host of planned activities, aimed at getting children who are in a new environment (something with many children find threatening in and of itself) at the last minute to take their minds off their confusion and redirect attention to educational playtime.

Outside activities such as learning about wildflowers and catching butterflies in nets, mingle with inside activities such as finger painting. All activities are variable depending on what time of year it is, and what the weather is like outside, of course. The overall purpose of any drop in center activity is to take the child's mind off the scariness of a new situation, and instead distract them with something fun.

Because the children present at a drop in center fluctuate day-to-day, there is often not enough time to build meaningful personal relationships with each an every individual child. There will always be exceptions to the rule, and daycare centers that offer a drop in option are of course not included in this generalization. The policies in place at a drop-in center take into account the fact that kids will vary over time, and that the center must place flexibility of services over deeply established personal relationships with each child.

Remember, emergency childcare is just that, so have your paperwork filled out and your fees paid at your local drop in center, just in case you may one day have to use it.

Childcare Co-ops

Another way that "it takes a village to raise a child" is put into play in modern America is in the local childcare co-ops. What a childcare co-op is, is basically a collection of local childcare professionals, including babysitters, put together by a local organization devoted to organizing and managing social responsibility within the immediate community, such as a church, hospital, or neighborhood watch association.

Most co-ops have criteria that it's members offering services must adhere to, such as being over the age of 16, and passing a basic first aid course. Some co-ops take it upon themselves to teach a basic first aid/ emergency preparedness course for young people who want to join their co-op as babysitters for hire, and, when this type of course is offered, the people who take and pass it are usually admitted to the co-op's babysitting pool as a matter of course.

Unlike the cyber-nanny trend that is terrorizing our neighborhoods (there will be more on cyber-nanny databases and pitfalls in the cyber-nanny section) co-ops are usually dedicated to presenting families with qualified babysitters who are answerable to the co-op if something goes extremely wrong, or if a babysitter's behavior is in breach of the basic co-op criteria for behavior. Much like ethics boards review health care workers' behaviors on-the-job, and so everyone knows that the most well-paid doctor is still answerable to the ethics review board for questionable behavior, so, too, is the babysitter answerable to the childcare co-op. This clearly drawn line in the sand makes personal responsibility a community value, rather than just a hoped-for feature of common sense, as it is in cyber-nanny databases.

Mother's helpers and play groups may be birthed from co-ops, with mother's helpers discussed in their own section of this booklet. Play groups are often composed of several parents who work part time, who get together during their time off to socialize with other parents, and have their children socialize with one another. The ages of the children in a playgroup can range from infants, to toddlers, to preschool aged children, and the size of a play group can also vary greatly group to group.

In play groups, often parents will set up a schedule where each parent involved in the play group watches the children in the group for a certain number of hours on certain days. This allows other parents in the group to work, go on errands, and so on. Since the group is composed of people who are sharing childcare in exchange for receiving childcare from the other members of the group, it's essentially a free form of childcare, and as such is affordable.

Another advantage of the play group is that the parents will normally be associated with each other through the social organization, such as church or neighborhood watch committee, that formed the co-op that spawned the play group. This means that the parents involved will most likely share some core values and belief systems that other parents in the groups will feel comfortable exposing their children to. The constant neighborly interaction among the adults in play groups and co-ops is one of the main reasons that such childcare alternatives are not only financially feasible, but earn top marks in safety for the children involved as well.

Cyber-nanny

This childcare "option" is an altogether bad idea, brought to you by the tech generation.

In theory, it's a nice idea. Gather a database of all the available babysitters in an area, list them according to time preference, (such as: Is this a weekends-only babysitter? Is this babysitter available for full time hours per week? and so on) and then make that list available to anyone who is looking for a babysitter. There are national and local databases, which means that the local data is organized on national and local levels, but both types provide local sitters for parents in need of childcare. Some even let parents list "sitters wanted" ads if they want to.

What problems could there possibly be? It sounds altogether progressive, doesn't it?

This is because the cyber-nanny's biggest flaw is it's hidden flaw: the lists are not composed of people who have been screened and found to not have a criminal background, history of domestic violence, etc, they are simply lists of everyone in an area who is interested in picking up a babysitting gig. Worse, since each sitter writes his or her own listing, the predators are likely to have very enticing, professional-looking profiles on these cites.

Kind of makes the bottom of your stomach feel cold and numb, like you're about to be sick, doesn't it?

There are some efforts being made to screen potential sitters on the local level, but these efforts are few and far between. By and large, the cyber-nanny lists are just dog piles of potential baby sitters, where parents pick and choose based on whoever looks good, kind of like picking out produce at a supermarket.

The thing is, in the supermarket, the produce has to meet certain standards -it can't be sold if it's rotten, for example- whereas in these databases, there are no standards save whatever ones the parents bring with them to their keyboards when they look through the lists.

There is no way to tell if someone is lying, either - have you ever cut into a cantaloupe just to find the inside swimming with maggots, and rotting away? Didn't it look so fresh and delicious just an hour ago, when you bought it, before you cut it open? Things like that aren't supposed to happen; we trust our grocery store not to sell us rotten, poisoned, or expired food, and we pay them good money because we trust them.

Unfortunately, a computerized data base lends an air of credibility and professionalism to the babysitters listed on it that is entirely false in it's nature. We think we are trusting someone responsible with our children, but, the fact is, there is no way to cut through the attractive profile, to see if the flesh inside of the fruit is fresh and edible, until we have already bought the sitter's services. By the time we see the maggots, it may already be too late.

If you are looking for a local babysitter, perhaps thinking of the traditional junior high school kid who wants to earn a little money but isn't old enough to work yet, so that you can have a night to yourself once a week or so, ask your neighbors who have children who the good ones are. Their recommendations are far superior to the pseudo-professionalism of the dog pile database, as they will be based on real interactions with the babysitters they are talking about, and fellow parents have no reasons to lie or hide things about the sitter they choose to rely on themselves.

The worst that can happen if you trust word of mouth is that you might wind up competing with your neighbors for the most reliable, affordable, and popular sitters. That's a livable outcome, since most places have more than one teen or pre-teen looking for work as a baby sitter. If you don't get your first choice, your next in line may cost a couple dollars more, or maybe the kids don't like her quite as much, or maybe you need to commit to a fixed schedule in order to keep a good one. There will always be runners-up who are still perfectly safe and sane choices, sitters who someone in the neighborhood knows personally and can vouch for.

A so-so babysitter that's a little more expensive, and that the kids kind of like, is the worse case scenario when you go by word of mouth. This is still a world away from allowing a potential predator into your house, so beware cyber nannies, and talk to your neighbors and friends.

Licensed vs Unlicensed In Home Childcare

Now that we've discussed the various forms of childcare that are available and popular in America today, we should look at some of the potentially major differences between a licensed and an unlicensed in home childcare facility.

If you remember from it's section, in home childcare is when a child is brought to the home of the childcare worker, and is taken care of for the parents' working day there, usually in a group with other children who are being similarly cared for.

But what are some of the deeper questions parents should be asking the in home childcare workers before leaving their children with such a person?

The first, and arguably most important question, is:

Is this particular in home childcare worker licensed?

Whether or not an in home childcare worker is licensed is the single biggest selling point or red flag when dealing with an in home childcare facility. Most states have laws governing licensed in home childcare facilities, laws that are set up for the protection and safety of the children who go there.

One such law is a ratio of children to workers that cannot be exceeded in that particular area. For example, if the ratio in Alabama for a licensed in home childcare facility is 1:5, that means that for every 5 children that are cared for in the facility, there must be at least one adult worker on the books who is there to supervise the children during the normal hours of operation. Unlicensed centers don't need to pay attention to state ratios, and so the probability that there will be fewer adults present than what the state considers optimal is greatly increased in an unlicensed in home childcare facility.

Another law in most states requires licensed in home childcare facilities to have at least one person certified in Basic First Aid on duty during the working day. The American Red Cross offers literature and day long courses for the parent who would like to be able to question the person giving this medical care more intimately. In an unlicensed center, there is, of course, no requirement, and so it is very important to ask questions about emergency medical care available on-site if a facility is being considered.

Finally, there is a law in most states that requires licensed in home childcare facilities to employ workers who can pass a criminal background check, and to fire immediately anyone who is found to have any sort of violent criminal past, or who have past or current drug charges against them. This may seem like common sense, but ask yourself this question: are you willing to gamble with your child's safety by sending him or her to an unlicensed worker in an unlicensed facility that didn't ever and does not now need to have their employees pass such a background check?

If so, what did it take for your in-home care provider to gain licensure?

In addition to background checks, Basic First Aid certification, and proper caregiver to child ratios, licensed facilities must maintain strict standards of cleanliness and adequate home planning; undergo inspections from agency representatives to gain and maintain their license, including bi-yearly renewals; employ workers who are competent to deal with children in a primary care environment; strictly adhere to fire codes and other safety codes while the center is operational; be transparent about who will be in the home during childcare hours and absolutely bar entrance to anyone unsuitable for the environment, such as a registered sex offender; and take childcare and development classes to further understanding and awareness of the children left in the worker's supervision.

While the license is in place, centers are answerable to higher authorities for all actions -including negligent inactions- taken while children are present at the in home care facility. If you feel that a licensed facility isn't complying with the standards set forth to protect children in the in home environment, formal complaints can be made to state licensing boards by anyone who is concerned for the well being of the children in such a center.

If not, were they licensed at one time, and lost licensure?

If so, how did they lose it, are they working to get it back, and what are the relevant details regarding the loss? Because there are such strict standards, licensure is occasionally revoked until problems are solved in a given in home childcare facility.

Sometimes, the reasons for the removal of a legitimate license are simple and easily fixed, such as if a facility forgot to drop off renewal paperwork; was slightly over in their childcare worker to child ratios (say a legal ratio of 1:5 was accidentally expanded in practice to 1:7, for example); or was lax in taking a recertification or ongoing education course. In such simple cases as the ones listed above, regaining the license can be as easy as filing the paperwork and paying a late fee; hiring more workers for the in home childcare center; and taking annual trainings under a worker's hours are back up to what they should be, respectively.

However, sometimes in home childcare facilities lose their licenses for reasons that are less easily fixed, which may be why a center in currently running without a license. Unlike medical doctors and psychologists, licensure removal doesn't necessarily equate to nonworking status at an in home childcare center. There could potentially be a very serious legal breach that could potentially result in an injury to a child present at the facility, and these types of breaches aren't going to be advertised at the open houses unless they are asked about and details are pushed for. Always ensure that the in home childcare facility you leave your child with is working towards licensure, and keep on top of them regarding their time line: if they say their inspection is in two months, then, two months later, ask how the inspection went, and find out how the process towards the facility becoming licensed is running along.

If it seems to you that too much time is passing, or that the answers being given are inadequate, remove your child from the potentially harmful environment and relocate them to a center that already holds a license.

If your in home childcare worker was never licensed, why not, and are they working towards licensure now?

In some cases, the in home childcare center has never been licensed, the most usual reason being that the business is just starting up. Working with a new center that doesn't have an established reputation, but whose workers are part of a neighborhood co-op, or something similar, is a perfectly understandable reason why an in home childcare facility might not have it's license yet, although many wait to open their doors until the license is framed and on the wall. In such situations of it simply being a process in the works, ask questions, and stay on task with the center's time line for licensure, keeping the lines of communication between center and parents open as much as possible, as mentioned above.

Also as mentioned above, remove your child immediately if the answers to your questions don't satisfy. Social embarrassment is a small price to pay to keep your child safe, and there are many "scam" in home childcare centers who are "waiting for their license" and have been doing so for months or even years, without having submitted the proper paperwork or made the necessary adjustments to the in home environment to ever qualify. If you notice obvious substandard cleanliness, or areas of potential fire hazards, the rule of thumb is that there will be others that are not seen and noticed. Bring your childcare worker's attention to such infractions immediately; if they are legitimately looking for licensure, they will thank you for pointing them out. If they get snarly or otherwise irate at your comments, you may want to think about relocating your child until their licensure officially goes through.

Talking to parents about the career journey of their worker, and subsequent decision to follow a career in the childcare field.

There are many traits that people who are good at working with children have in common, such as patience, a respectful nature, and good organizational skills. When choosing a childcare setting, it is often the childcare worker who ultimately sells or deflates the parents' decision on where and who to go with. This is not only true with au pairs, nannies, and co-ops, but also with in home care, daycare facilities, and preschools.

Establishing open lines of communication between childcare facilities, workers, and parents should be a high priority on everyone's to do list. As parents, taking the time to discuss some of the more personal reasons that a preschool teacher, or a nanny, or another form of childcare worker, has chosen that particular career path, and where the path might lead them in the future in terms of personal goals, can go a long way towards striking up a bond with your child's care giver or care givers, and is invaluable as a soothing balm to a parent's nerves when leaving a child in a new environment for the first time.

We Want Your Feedback on This Book!

Our main purpose is to make sure that our readers get value from the books we publish and that they have a good experience with all of our products. We are always working to improve our books and other products with every revision and update.

Every piece of feedback makes a difference in this process. And we would appreciate yours as well - whether it is good or bad.

Please take one minute to let us know what you thought by following this link:

http://checkmatemg.com/feedbackchildcare

Printed in Great Britain
by Amazon.co.uk, Ltd.,
Marston Gate.